POLITICAL ACTION

A Bible study by
CHARLES COLSON
with RON KLUG

NAVPRESS
A MINISTRY OF THE NAVIGATORS
P.O. BOX 6000, COLORADO SPRINGS, COLORADO 80934

The Navigators is an international Christian organization. Jesus Christ gave His followers the Great Commission to go and make disciples (Matthew 28:19). The aim of The Navigators is to help fulfill that commission by multiplying laborers for Christ in every nation.

NavPress is the publishing ministry of The Navigators. NavPress publications are tools to help Christians grow. Although publications alone cannot make disciples or change lives, they can help believers learn biblical discipleship, and apply what they learn to their lives and ministries.

© 1988 by Charles Colson
All rights reserved, including translation
ISBN 08910-92552

Photography: Mark Reis

This study includes excerpts from various books by Charles Colson. Study questions and suggestions for group activities were compiled by Ron Klug.

Grateful acknowledgment is made to the following publishers for permission to reprint excerpts from selected books by Charles Colson: *Who Speaks for God?*, © 1985, Crossway Books, Westchester, Ill., and *Kingdoms in Conflict*, © 1987, William Morrow/Zondervan Publishing House, New York/Grand Rapids, Mich.

Scripture quotations in this publication are from the *Holy Bible: New International Version* (NIV). Copyright © 1973, 1978, 1984, International Bible Society. Used by permission of Zondervan Bible Publishers.

Printed in the United States of America

Contents

Contents

Author

Charles Colson received his bachelor's degree from Brown University and his law degree from George Washington University. From 1969-1973 he served as special counsel to President Richard M. Nixon. He pleaded guilty to charges related to Watergate in 1974 and served seven months in prison. He is now chairman of Prison Fellowship Ministries, a Washington, D.C.-based organization that he founded in 1976.

Colson is the author of several books, including *Born Again* (Chosen Books, 1976), *Life Sentence* (Chosen Books, 1979), *Loving God* (Zondervan Publishing Co., 1983), *Who Speaks for God?* (Crossway Books, 1985), and *Kingdoms in Conflict* (Morrow/Zondervan Publishing Co., 1987). He is also a frequent contributor to magazines and journals. All of his speaking fees and book royalties are donated to further the work of Prison Fellowship Ministries, P.O. Box 17500, Washington, DC 20041, (703) 478-0100.

Preface

One of the greatest challenges Christians face is that of our dual citizenship: How do we live as citizens of both the Kingdom of God and of the kingdoms of this world?

This tension runs like an unbroken thread through the centuries. The early Christians worshiped a King other than Caesar, and as a result were cast into the lions' den. Not for religious reasons—Rome, after all, was a land of many gods—but because they refused to worship the emperor.

Since then Christians have formed unholy alliances with Caesar, merging the institutions of church and state; or they have gone to the other extreme, divorcing themselves completely from government, cloistered away from responsible involvement in the world. It has never been simple for citizens of the two kingdoms to render to Caesar what is Caesar's and to God what is God's.

Certainly it is not easy today. Rome's arenas may have crumbled, but the lions are still prowling. The modern state—in both its totalitarian and democratic forms—has grown in power and influence, tending by its very nature to dominate all areas of life, and thus to steadily encroach on religious values.

The questions facing Christians are many. How do we fulfill our responsibilities to church and state? What are their separate God-ordained roles? Can we work through political channels for justice and righteousness—or is politics inherently corrupting?

A period in the late eighteenth and early nineteenth centuries offers an instructive and inspiring example for us today. Believers in England, their hearts strangely warmed by Wesley's revivals and their consciences pierced by the barbarism of the slave trade and other injustices against the weak and helpless, were stirred to political action. They rallied grassroots citizens' groups; they fought for humane legislation in the halls of government.

Their opponents were infuriated. "Things have come to a pretty pass when religion is allowed to invade public life," sniffed one Lord Melbourne. But in spite of the opposition of those who saw no connection between private belief and public action, Christians gave leadership to some of the most sweeping reforms of modern times.

Today we hear many Lord Melbournes decrying religiously induced involvement in public life. Some candidates take pains to reassure voters that their faith will have no bearing on their official conduct. The media and the courts are zealous proponents of that same viewpoint, steadily stripping the public square naked of transcendent values.

The call for Christians today is to respond vigorously and responsibly, to bring a Christian witness to modern American society. We must be what Augustine called "the best of citizens," serving our neighbors and the common good out of the love of God, being salt and light in these dark times.

But to do so, we must avoid two traps. First, we must not privatize our faith by withdrawing from the public arena altogether. Of what earthly good is the Kingdom then?

Second, we must not politicize our faith, marrying the values of the Kingdom of God to some particular political agenda. Both of these traps are equally dangerous; neither has anything to do with historic Christianity and the lordship of Jesus Christ.

It is my prayer that this study will help you discover the biblical mandates concerning our dual citizenship in the Kingdom of God and the kingdoms of man, and to sense God's particular call to you to bring His values to bear on the community of which you are a part. This process involves tough questions and prayerful responses. There are no easy formulas or pat answers. But it is in the process of thinking through these issues that we discover how to truly make witness of the truth of the Kingdom of God to a desperately needy world.

Introduction from the Publisher

"Why does NavPress want to publish a series of Bible studies by Charles Colson?"

This is the question Charles Colson asked of us when we proposed the idea to him.

The answer begins with Jesus' words in Luke 11:28— "Blessed . . . are those who hear the word of God and obey it." Such obedience should result in a vigorous spiritual life which impacts the world around it.

Yet researcher George Barna has made the disturbing observation that Americans who profess a continuing commitment to Jesus Christ evidence few lifestyle differences from nonbelievers. In terms of surveyable attitudes and behavior patterns—even in such areas as divorce, child abuse, materialism, and civic responsibility—the Body of Christ in the Unites States looks nearly identical to secular society.

Certainly the problem is not a lack of biblical preaching and teaching. God has raised up many gifted men and women in our time who are regularly bringing His Word to His people through a variety of media.

Perhaps part of the problem is that we are simply not doing what we already know to do. We do not heed Paul's command to the Philippians to put into practice what we learn or receive. Superficial devotion characterizes many segments of American Christianity.

We in NavPress desire to play a strategic part in encouraging the Church toward a vigorous obedience to the Word of God, resulting in a genuine renewal that will strengthen and deepen our impact on society. We believe that we can do this by linking up our resources with the gifted teachers and prophets whom God has raised up in our time—and offering their teaching in a form that will stimulate deeper and more lasting obedience to our Lord Jesus Christ.

We feel that the Christian small group is an outstanding instrument for this purpose. As a publisher of Bible studies, we are inevitably biased in favor of small groups. However, we have not yet seen a more effective teaching medium through which to generate real change in a person's life. The small group provides accountability, encouragement, fellowship in God's Word, and the power of warm and living spiritual unity, support, and edification so important to the life of the church.

Our strategic aim in this and succeeding studies is to help shape the messages of Charles Colson, whom God has remarkably gifted and empowered for ministry to this generation, into effective tools for small group use. Our desire is that these guides will further deepen and make practical his prophetic and far-reaching call to revolutionary Christian living.

How to Use This Guide

How can Christians live as citizens of the Kingdom of God in
the kingdoms of this world?
Should Christians be involved in politics?
What does the separation of church and state involve?
In a pluralistic society should Christians seek to impose Chris-
tian values on nonChristians?

This study guide is designed to help you seek—and find—
answers to questions like these. It can be used by individuals, but
it will offer the greatest benefits when used in a small group set-
ting, where insights can be shared, questions answered, and differing viewpoints explored. A small group can also help foster
commitment and self-discipline, as members support and
encourage each other in putting biblical teachings into practice.
In a small group Christians can join together in worship and
prayer.

Each session in this study guide is divided into six parts.

1. *Opening Reflection.* Each session begins with an excerpt
from the author's writings. Before you read it, ask the Holy Spirit
to open your mind to His truth. When you come together as a
group, you may want to read it aloud. The questions that immediately follow it, in the "Opening Reflection" section, are to help
you reflect on its meaning and implications. Answer these questions in your personal study, and then discuss them in your
group. Use this discussion as a warmup for the next part of your
session, which will explore issues arising from key Scripture
passages.

2. *Turning to the Scriptures.* If you are part of a study group,
do your own study first, before the meeting. Allow at least an
hour for this preparation. Some of the questions ask you to look
at what the Bible *says.* Others direct you to think about what the

11

Bible *means.* Still others encourage you to *apply* the Scriptures to your own life and the life of your community.

When you come together as a group, discuss your answers. Come with the intention of learning from one another. The proper attitude is one of humility before God's Word and one another.

Some of the issues discussed in this study are emotionally charged for many people. Remember that in a Christian group, you are gathering as brothers and sisters in Christ, seeking His lordship. Encourage the expression of differing viewpoints. Always come back to the question, "What is God saying to us through His Word?"

It will probably be helpful to designate a leader to guide the discussion. If the group begins to get too far off the track, the leader can gently bring it back to the Bible study or the issues at hand.

3. *For Further Reflection.* Following the Bible study are quotations from Charles Colson and other Christian writers. Use these excerpts as springboards for your thinking and discussion. In your private study, read them slowly and thoughtfully, jotting down any questions or thoughts you have. Share these notes in your group meeting.

4. *Moving into Action.* "Do not merely listen to the word, and so deceive yourselves. Do what it says," wrote the Apostle James (James 1:22). And Jesus gave us His promise, "Everyone who hears these words of mine and puts them into practice is like a wise man who built his house on the rock" (Matthew 7:24).

After reflecting on the Bible and selected Christian writings, we move into action, putting God's Word into practice and deepening our learning. These actions can then lead to further reflection.

It is important that you as an individual and as a group take at least some of these actions. However, don't feel that you have to do them all. Group members can choose from among the activities, working as individuals, in pairs, or as a subgroup. Some activities would be appropriate for the whole group.

Schedule time for these activities between your group meetings. When you meet as a group, share what you did and your reactions to it. This will provide an excellent opportunity for you to learn from one another.

5. *Ideas for Group Worship.* Conclude your group meeting with worship. (You may also wish to end your personal study with prayer and praise.) Worship gives glory to God and helps establish group unity and harmony by creating a common focus on the Lord. Communal prayer and worship can reduce or even eliminate any tensions that have built up in the group.

Feel free to adapt the worship suggestions to your particular group. You may, for example, want to do more singing. Perhaps one person in the group could serve as worship leader, or leadership could be rotated.

6. *Reading Resources.* Optional resources are suggested at the end of each session for those who wish to dig more deeply into a topic.

The Coming of the Kingdom

*Because of the nature of the King and the price He paid for His Kingdom, much is required of its citizens, and Jesus made these demands of the Kingdom clear. Through the centuries, however, many of His followers have watered down His teaching, stripped away His demands for the building of a righteous society, and preached an insipid religion concerned only with personal benefits. This distorted view portrays Christianity not as the powerful source of spiritual rebirth and the mediating force for justice, mercy, and love in the world, but as the ultimate self-fulfillment plan. The gospel is not a release for the captives, but confidence for the shy. It is the spiritual equivalent of racy sports cars, designer clothes, and Gordon's Gin—a commodity to help one get more out of life.

Many humanists have failed to understand human nature. But many Christians have failed also—failed to understand the utterly radical nature of the central message of Christianity. Other great leaders have expounded creeds, philosophies, and mystical visions. Many are wise and moral, but they are only belief systems: rules to live by, value codes. Men and women require more than rules; they require what Jesus' message of the Kingdom uniquely provides: answers to their most basic needs.

What are these needs?

To know God. "The heart of man is restless until it finds its rest in Thee." With these simple words Augustine expressed man's most primal yearning—the need to know God. In announcing His messiahship Jesus was saying that God's love and just rule had come to earth—in Him. Men and women would thereafter be able to find rest not in a law they could never hope to fulfill, but in the actual person of

Jesus Christ.

To find salvation. But how does one come to a personal relationship with this Christ? That is the archetypal question asked by the apostle Paul's jailer: "What must I do to be saved?"

Because we interpret it from our perspective and not God's, salvation has always been misunderstood. The Jew wanted salvation from his oppressor, the Roman centurion. Instead, Christ came to save him from a much greater oppressor—the sin within him.

Sin is essentially rebellion against the rule of God. This is why Jesus coupled the message of the Kingdom with the call to repent and believe. Faith and repentance, the opposite of rebellion, are the necessary human responses to the divine initiative of spiritual rebirth, resulting in salvation.

When Christ first used the term *born again,* it was not the evangelical cliché or secular slur it is today. He used it in a late-night conversation with Nicodemus, a member of the Jewish religious community, telling him it was the key to entering into the Kingdom of God. Imagine the shock of the religious elite when they heard Jesus' words: Salvation was not to be found in proud piety or scrupulous adherence to religious rules, but in a turning from evil and humble faith in One greater than oneself. Just as a person is born physically in a particular nation, so he or she is born spiritually by submitting to God's rule in His holy nation.

To find meaning. This relationship with God meets man's deepest psychological need. As we have already seen, human beings cannot live in a vacuum. We are not a chance collision of atoms in an indifferent universe or islands amid cold currents of modern culture. We each have a personal purpose in history, which is to be found under the purposeful rule of God, as a beloved citizen of His Kingdom.

To find authority. Christianity is more than simply a relationship between man and God, however. The Kingdom of God embraces every aspect of life: ethical, spiritual, and temporal, and it determines the "pattern, purpose and dynamic by which God orders life of the heavenly polis in this world."

Kingdoms in Conflict

Opening Reflection

1. What basic human needs are met by Jesus' message of the Kingdom of God?

2. Although Jesus made clear the nature of citizenship in His Kingdom, "many of His followers have watered down His teaching, stripped away His demands for the building of a righteous society, and preached an insipid religion concerned only with personal benefits." Do you agree? Why or why not?

Turning to the Scriptures

3. Read Matthew 3:1-6.

a. What announcement did John the Baptist make?

b. What do you understand by the term "the kingdom of heaven"? (You may want to consult a Bible dictionary or commentary for additional insights.)

c. What response to his announcement did John look for?

4.   a. When Jesus began to preach, what was His main theme (Matthew 4:12-25)?

Repent for The
        Kingdom of Heaven is near

b. With what actions did Jesus accompany His proclamation of the Kingdom?

miracles

5. Read Matthew 8:5-13. In Jesus' day many Jews identified the Kingdom of God with the nation of Israel. How did Jesus expand their understanding of the extent of His Kingdom in His response to the centurion?

He performed a miracle of healing
on a non-Jew.

6. Jesus used many parables or pictures to help His disciples—
and us—understand the Kingdom He came to inaugurate. In
each passage listed below, identify the major picture or metaphor
and briefly note the main point Jesus is teaching about His
Kingdom.

Picture	Main teaching
Matthew 13:31-32 Mustard seed becomes tree	something very small grows into a very large source of life when planted/nutured
Matthew 13:44 Treasure in the field	Don't hid the Lord or you will pay deatly to get him back.
Matthew 18:21-35	
Matthew 20:1-16	

Picture	Main teaching
Matthew 21:33–46	
Matthew 22:1-14	

7. Read Matthew 18:1-9.

    a. When Jesus' disciples asked who would be greatest in His Kingdom, how did Jesus answer them?

    b. In what ways might a child serve as an illustration of what it means to be a member of Christ's Kingdom?

8. a. When Jesus sent His disciples out to evangelize, what was the main thrust of their witness (Luke 9:1-2)?

b. What are the implications of this passage for our own efforts at evangelism?

9. Read Mark 10:17-25.

a. Why was the young man unable to accept Jesus' invitation to the Kingdom of God?

b. Why might it be difficult for a person who is rich (materially or religiously) to enter the Kingdom of God?

10. a. Are you a citizen of the Kingdom Jesus came to inaugurate?

yes ☐   no ☐   don't know ☐

b. If so, how did you become one?

c. If not, what prevents you from becoming a member of Christ's Kingdom?

11. Read Matthew 6:25-34. Jesus commanded, "Seek first his kingdom and his righteousness." What does it mean for you to seek God's Kingdom first in each of these life areas:

Your family life

Your job

Your time commitments

Your life goals

Your political involvement

Your friendships

12. Take a few minutes to list any questions you have after working through this first chapter. The quotations in the following section, "For Further Reflection," may throw some light on your questions. You might also find answers in some of the resources listed in the bibliography at the end of this chapter. Bring any remaining questions to your next group session, or ask for help from a friend or trusted acquaintance.

For Further Reflection

Meditate on the following statements in light of the Bible study
you have just done. Write down any thoughts or questions you
may have. If you are part of a study group, share your reflections
in the group.

*The two Testaments are organically linked to each other. The rela-
tionship between them is neither one of upward development nor of
contrast; it is one of beginning and completion, of hope and fulfillment.* And the bond that binds them together is the dynamic concept of the rule of God. *There is indeed a "new thing" in the New
Testament, but it lies precisely here. The Old Testament is illumined
with the hope of the coming Kingdom, and the same Kingdom lies at
the heart of the New Testament as well. But the New Testament has
introduced what we might call a tremendously significant change of
tense. To the Old Testament the fruition and victory of God's Kingdom was always a future, indeed an eschatological thing, and must
always be spoken of in the future tense: "Behold, the days are coming"; "It shall come to pass in those days." But in the New Testament we encounter a change: the tense is a resounding present
indicative—the Kingdom is here! And that is a very "new thing"
indeed: it is gospel—the good news that God has acted.*

John Bright,
The Kingdom of God

*The Kingdom of God embraces every aspect of life: ethical, spiritual,
and temporal, and it determines the "pattern, purpose and dynamic
by which God orders life of the heavenly polis in this world."*

*In announcing this all-encompassing Kingdom, Jesus was not
using a clever metaphor; He was expressing the literal theme of Jewish history—that God was King and the people were His subjects.
This tradition dated back to the days of Abraham and the patriarchs
when God made His original covenant with the Jews to be His "holy
nation."*

*David, the first great king of the Jews, consolidated a visible
kingdom for the people of God, but it was to be only a reflection of
the ultimate rule of God, their true king. From David, the scepter
passed to his son Solomon, and on through a succession of rulers,
some good, some bad, but all serving as a link between God and His
subjects. Later, when the Jews were conquered and sent into exile,*

*prophets promised the coming of Messiah and the eventual establish-
ment of the Kingdom of God. Christ was the fulfillment of that proph-
ecy; He was the final king in David's royal line. But Jesus was not
just a king for Israel; He was a King for all people.*

Charles Colson,
Kingdoms in Conflict

*The New Testament's use of the political term "kingdom" to de-
scribe the sum of God's redemptive purposes indicates that the total
transformation of all things which God intends for his creation
includes a transformation of the political realm as well as other
realms. The first coming of the Son of Man into the world was not
only a challenge to individual sinners and ecclesiastical institutions;
it was a threat to the political status quo. It was politicians who
sought to kill Jesus shortly after he was born, and it was politicians
who finally had a hand in his death.*

Richard Mouw,
Political Evangelism

*To be a citizen of the Kingdom means that God's will is our will, for
that is the way it was for Jesus all his days. Often Jesus used to go
away to be alone with God; before every great act and decision and
crisis in his life he prayed. Always he was asking what God wanted
him to do. When we, by his help, forget ourselves and think only of
God we, too, will be citizens of the Kingdom.*
*In Jesus the Kingdom was fully realised because of all people, he
alone perfectly carried out the will of God. In Jesus God came and
lived this life and himself fulfilled his own commandments and laws.
In Jesus we see that for a boy the Kingdom means obedience, constant
growth in knowledge and in goodness, so that we please God better
every day. In Jesus we see that for a workman the Kingdom means
putting our best into every task. In Jesus we see that for a man the
Kingdom means serving men and obeying God all the days of his life.*

William Barclay,
The King and His Kingdom

Jesus said that the Kingdom of God has come in Him. *The kingdom
is a rule, not a realm. It is not a physical territory, but the reign of
God over all. When we are followers of Christ, we pledge allegiance
to a new set of values, a different set of citizenship requirements.*

Living as a citizen of the Kingdom of God in the midst of the decaying kingdoms of the world—that to me is the great challenge for Christians today—that is how we make a difference.

Charles Colson in
Charisma and Christian Life

Moving into Action

Now is the time to begin putting into action what you have learned. This important step will help you continue and deepen your learning. If you are part of a group, divide up the action steps in this and the following sessions. You can work as individuals, in pairs, or in small groups. Be prepared to report back to the whole group at your next meeting.

1. Using a concordance and/or Bible dictionary, do a study of the term "Kingdom of God."

2. Ask a Christian who serves in government to speak to your group about how the Christian faith influences his or her work. Or, interview a person and report back to your group.

3. Read John Bright's book *The Kingdom of God* and give a brief report to your group.

4. Throughout this study you will be thinking about the ways in which the Christian faith informs political and social issues. Be on the alert for newspaper and magazine articles that discuss these issues. Watch for articles that tell what Christians are doing in the political realm. Clip or photocopy articles and share them with the group. All members of the group may wish to participate in this activity.

Ideas for Group Worship

Sing a hymn that praises Jesus as King, like "O Worship the King," "Crown Him with Many Crowns," or "I Love Thy Kingdom, Lord." Ask God to bless your study and give you new insights into His Kingdom and your role in it.

Reading Resources

William Barclay, *The King and His Kingdom* (Philadelphia: Westminster Press, 1968).

John Bright, *The Kingdom of God* (New York and Nashville: Abingdon/Cokesbury, 1953).

Charles Colson, *Kingdoms in Conflict* (New York/Grand Rapids: William Morrow/Zondervan Publishing House, 1987).

Living Between the Times

I've used this message of human liberation from the Gospel of Luke [Luke 4:18-19] countless times as the centerpiece of my message to prisoners. "He has sent me to proclaim freedom for the prisoners . . . to release the oppressed. . . ." It speaks of men and women set free by the good news of the gospel. Not until I began to research this book did I understand its wider significance.

Of all the Scriptures Jesus might have read, He chose the one that unmistakably announced the coming of the Kingdom of God. Furthermore, the listening Jews understood that in this particular passage of Isaiah, the one speaking *is* the messenger—the Messiah who ushers in the Kingdom era. To those in that synagogue, Jesus' words could only mean that He was claiming to be the Messiah. And if that was true, the Kingdom of Heaven had become a present reality.

One reason I, like many others, missed this deeper meaning of Christ's radical declaration is that I had always read the term *kingdom* metaphorically. Like the Jews in that Nazareth synagogue, most of us think of kingdoms as geographic entities, physical realms with boundaries and defenses and treasuries. But the Kingdom of God is a rule, not a realm. It is the declaration of God's absolute sovereignty, of His total order of life in this world and the next.

Throughout His ministry, Jesus repeatedly returned to the Kingdom theme. In the Sermon on the Mount, He told His followers to "seek first his kingdom and his righteousness." He consistently defined His work as ushering in the Kingdom of God. Almost all of His parables focused on the Kingdom in one aspect or another, while His miracles authenticated His message. In converting water to wine, calming storms, multiplying loaves and fishes, healing the sick, and raising the dead, Jesus was not working magic to gather crowds; nor was He showing His power to gain credibility. He was demonstrating the reality of His rule. By exercising dominion over every phase of earthly existence, He revealed that in fact the Kingdom of God had come.

The Jews of first-century Palestine missed Christ's message because they, like many today, were conditioned to look for salvation in political solutions. More than anything else they wanted to be set free of Roman rule. They longed for a military messiah who would stamp out their hated oppressors. It is not surprising, then, that support for the Zealots was widespread.

The Zealot political vision was too narrow, however; for Jesus to embrace it would have been to limit the Kingdom of God to Israel. Though, ironically, Jesus was later tried and convicted as a Zealot, He dashed the hopes of those whose narrow political expectations blinded them to His real message.

The same could be said of the Jewish hierarchy. They might have welcomed Jesus because of their messianic expectations. Instead, they jealously guarded their own arrogant, self-righteous interpretation of the Jewish law, as well as the limited autonomy the Romans had given them.

Palestine's factions were embroiled in a struggle over the political and religious future of a limited ethnic group confined and defined by geographic borders. In pointing to a far larger Kingdom, Jesus was a leader without a constituency. Even His closest followers had times of doubt.

Another reason that the Jews missed the full significance of the message of the Kingdom of God was that Jesus spoke about a Kingdom that had come and a Kingdom that was still to come—one Kingdom in two stages. This still confuses people today. Perhaps a contemporary analogy will make it clearer.

Probably the most significant event in Europe during World War II was D-Day, June 6, 1944, when the Allied armies stormed the beaches of Normandy. That attack guaranteed the eventual destruction of the Axis powers in Europe. Though the war continued with seeming uncertainties along the way, the outcome was in fact determined. But it wasn't until May 8, 1945—VE Day—that the results of the forces set in motion eleven months earlier were realized.

We can compare this two-stage process to the strategy of the Kingdom of God.

A holy God would not take dominion over a sinful world. So He first sent His Son, Jesus Christ, to die on the cross to pay the debt for man's sin and thereby provide for men and women to be made holy and fit for God's rule. To extend our war analogy, Christ's death and resurrection—the D-Day of human history—assure His ultimate victory. But we are still on the beaches. The enemy has not yet been vanquished, and the fighting is still ugly. Christ's invasion has assured the ultimate outcome, however—victory for God and His people at some future date.

The second stage, which will take place when Christ returns, will assert God's rule over all the universe; His Kingdom will be visible without imperfection. At that time there will be a final judgment of all people, peace on earth, and the restoration of harmony unknown since Eden.

Many soldiers died to bring about the victory in Europe. But in the Kingdom of God, it was the death of the King that assured the victory. And this leads to the third reason that the Kingdom is often misunderstood: the nature of the King Himself.

What king would ever sacrifice himself for his people? Kings sacrifice their subjects, not themselves. What king would wash his servants' feet, as Jesus did, or freely befriend his lowest subjects? Potentates maintain the mystique of leadership by keeping a distance from those they rule. A certain grandeur seems to robe those who occupy high office.

I vividly recall a glimpse of this from my White House days. One brisk December night as I accompanied the president from the Oval Office in the West Wing of the White House to the Residence, Mr. Nixon was musing about what people wanted in their leaders. He slowed a moment, looking into the distance across the South Lawn, and said, "The people really want a leader a little bigger than themselves, don't they, Chuck?" I agreed. "I mean someone like de Gaulle," he continued. "There's a certain aloofness, a power that's exuded by great men that people feel and want to follow."

Jesus Christ exhibited none of this self-conscious aloofness. He served others first; He spoke to those to whom no one spoke; He dined with the lowest members of society; He touched the untouchables. He had no throne, no crown, no bevy of servants or armored guards. A borrowed manger and a borrowed tomb framed His earthly life.

Kings and presidents and prime ministers surround themselves with minions who rush ahead, swing the doors wide, and stand at attention as they wait for the great to pass. Jesus said that He Himself stands at the door and knocks, patiently waiting to enter our lives.

Kingdoms in Conflict

Opening Reflection

1. When Jesus announced that the Kingdom of God had arrived, many people did not accept His message. What misunderstandings caused them to miss the significance of Christ's life and message?

2. How did Jesus' nature as the King differ from the world's conception of a leader?

3. "The Kingdom of God is a rule, not a realm." What does this statement imply about the nature and presence of the Kingdom?

4. Look back at the comparison of Christ's death and resurrection to D-Day of WWII. How does this analogy help us understand the fact that the Kingdom has already come yet is still to come?

Turning to the Scriptures
5. In the first session we learned how the Kingdom of God arrived in the life of Jesus. Yet in the Lord's Prayer, Jesus taught us to pray, "Thy Kingdom come" (Matthew 6:10). Why do you think Jesus taught this prayer when He was also proclaiming that the Kingdom had come?

6. Read 1 Corinthians 15:20-28. What event do you see foretold in verse 24?

7.   a. Summarize the parable of Jesus recorded in Matthew 25:1-13.

   b. What attitude did Jesus wish to teach through this story?

8. Read Matthew 24:1-31. List some of the signs of the final coming of Christ's Kingdom.

9. Read 2 Peter 3:1-18.

    a. What advice did Peter give to believers who had to face skepticism about the final coming of Christ's Kingdom?

    b. According to Peter, why is the final coming delayed?

    c. What should our attitude be in the face of the coming destruction (verses 11 and 14)?

    d. What can we do to "speed the coming of the day"?

10. According to the parable of the net (Matthew 13:47-50), what will happen when Christ's Kingdom is fully present?

11. Read Matthew 25:31-46. When Jesus separates believers from unbelievers in the final judgment, with what actions will believers have demonstrated their faith?

12. Jesus told the parable of the weeds to describe conditions between the times of His two comings (Matthew 13:24-30).

a. Using the parable, and Jesus' own explanation in verses 36-43, identify the following:

The sower

The good seed

The weeds

The enemy

The harvest

The harvester

b. What does this parable suggest about our attitude toward nonChristians in the period "between the times"?

13. Paul wrote two letters to the Christians at Thessalonica, who were expecting the second coming of Christ's Kingdom to happen very soon. Read 1 Thessalonians 1:9-10.

a. What two actions does Paul encourage?

b. Why are both important for Christians?

14. List any questions that have come up in your study so far.

For Further Reflection

The Christian view of history is that the world is on its way to a final goal when the kingdoms of the world shall be the Kingdom of the Lord, and when Jesus shall return. When that day will be it is useless to speculate for even Jesus did not know its date. But though we cannot tell when it will come we can strive to be ready for its coming. The Kingdom is on the way for there are signs that God's will slowly but inevitably is conquering amongst men. The Kingdom is God's; without him nothing can happen; but we can hinder the coming of the kingdom by failing to give ourselves to him to use. And in the last analysis our first duty is to make him King of our hearts and Lord of our lives.

William Barclay,
The King and His Kingdom

The coming of the kingdom rests upon [God's] decision. He will select the time and the means. We cannot bring in the kingdom, but we can manifest the present reality of the kingdom by the power of his Spirit. We cannot build the kingdom, but we can herald and proclaim it. We can be stewards of the mystery of the gospel, but we cannot make the gospel successful. The gospel makes its own way in the world, for it is the very word of the all-powerful Son of God, Lord of the universe, Savior of humankind. But Christ has indicated that he wishes to speak his word through our broken words. It is through the folly of what we preach that Christ saves those who believe (cf. 1 Corinthians 1:21; Romans 10:17).

Donald Bloesch,
Crumbling Foundations

The Christian's hope is accompanied by the realization that the final victory is one God will bring about. The Scriptures promise that our acts of faithfulness relate to that final victory, but because we cannot always understand how, we must carry on, hoping that God will bless our efforts in such a way that they will relate to the final victory. The Christian is assured that his acts of obedience count for the coming of the Kingdom; but he cannot expect that they will count in accordance with the standards of success the world uses. Missionaries have spent entire lifetimes in Arab countries performing acts of mercy without ever seeing a person converted to Christianity. Yet in Christian terms their efforts count for the coming of the Kingdom of Jesus Christ. Similarly, the activities we pursue out of obedience to the political lordship of Christ count for the coming of his Kingdom.

Richard J. Mouw,
Political Evangelism

The Christian is essentially a man who lives in expectation. This expectation is directed towards the return of the Lord which accompanies the end of time, the Judgment, and proclaims the Kingdom of God. Thus one who knows that he has been saved by Christ is not a man jealously and timidly attached to a past, however glorious it may be. He does not cling to the past of his Church (tradition), nor even to the past life of Jesus Christ (on which, however, the certainty of his faith depends)—but he is a man of the future, not of a temporal and logical future, but of the eschaton, *of the coming break with this present world. Thus he looks forward to this moment, and for him all*

*facts acquire their value in the light of the coming Kingdom of God,
in the light of the Judgment, and the victory of God.*

Jacques Ellul,
The Presence of the Kingdom

*The Church must keep reminding us that God has his own program
mapped out for changing the world by the personal intervention of
Jesus Christ, who will return to establish the Kingdom of heaven on
earth. Yet simultaneously the Church must keep reminding us that
there is no biblical reason for concluding that enormous evils cannot
be significantly changed before our Lord comes back. The Church,
consequently, must keep reminding us as New Testament believers
that, whatever our political alignment, we ought to be spiritual sub-
versives, duplicating the redemptive radicalism of those first-century
Christians who were condemned for turning the world upside-down.
The Church must keep reminding us that we are God's saboteurs
working to bring about a revolution of faith and hope and love.*

Vernon Grounds in
Christianity Today

*The parable of the wheat and the tares is very important (Matthew
13:24-30). In the Gospel's context this parable prohibits any idealiz-
ing of ancient Israel and the longing for a return to a separate, pre-
exile state for God's people. It holds out no hope for a "Christian
state" in which Christians are organized into a separate political
existence from which all nonChristians are removed. The "tares"
(enemies of the kingdom) are to enjoy the same rain and sunshine, the
same care, the fertilizer, as the [followers of Christ] so long as both
are in the world together. . . .*

*A Christian view of justice, a Christian view of modern politics,
I believe, should be built on this understanding of God's gracious
patience during this age. It would not be* Christian *justice for Christians to enjoy some political privilege denied to others. A just state, a
just world, is one in which all citizens enjoy the same civil rights and
public care. Christian politics cannot be the church's attempt to control the state for it own well being; Christian politics cannot be con-
stituted by typical interest-group competition to make sure that
Christians get their way while others have to fend for themselves. . . .*

*My argument is on behalf of a principled pluralism in public
life, by which I mean the recognition that the God-ordained responsi-*

bility of government officials in modern states is to provide nondis-criminatory public justice for citizens of all faiths. This is not a tem-porary, pragmatic accommodation to the times simply because Chris-tians are too weak to gain control of government. Rather, it is an argument that democratic freedom for all citizens . . . grows directly, as a matter of principle, from a biblical view of the meaning of this age between the first and second comings of Christ. The "Christian" state is one that gives no special public privilege to Christian citizens but seeks justice for all as a matter of principle.

James W. Skillen,
"The Bible, Politics and Democracy"

We are forerunners of the kingdom: we witness to the kingdom, we manifest the values of the kingdom, we can be the influence of the kingdom in the world now. People get a taste of what the kingdom of God is by seeing how Christians live their lives and model those values.

Charles Colson in
Charisma and Christian Life

Moving into Action

Have group members report on the action steps they have taken since your last meeting. If someone has brought newspaper or magazine clippings, ask him or her to summarize them briefly. You might want to set them out on a table so interested members can review them after the session.

Choose from among the following action steps.

1. Do a study of the various Christian views regarding the second coming of Christ—the premillenial, postmillenial, and amillenial.

2. Read *The Meaning of the Millenium* by Robert G. Clouse and report to your group.

3. Read Charles Colson's *Kingdoms in Conflict* and report to your group.

4. Continue to look for newspaper and magazine articles dealing with the Christian and political issues.

Ideas for Group Worship

Sing or read a hymn together, like "In Christ There Is No East or West," "At the Name of Jesus," or "Jesus Shall Reign

Where'er the Sun."

Pray for the final coming of the Kingdom of God, and about any issues of concern that may have surfaced from the news clippings. Ask God to bless your study and the action steps you will take.

Reading Resources

William Barclay, *The King and His Kingdom* (Philadelphia: Westminster Press, 1968).

Donald Bloesch, *Crumbling Foundations* (Grand Rapids: Zondervan Publishing House, 1984).

John Bright, *The Kingdom of God* (New York and Nashville: Abingdon/Cokesbury, 1953).

Robert G. Clouse, *The Meaning of the Millenium: Four Views* (Downers Grove, Ill.: InterVarsity Press, 1977).

Charles Colson, *Kingdoms in Conflict* (New York/Grand Rapids: William Morrow/Zondervan Publishing House, 1987).

The Cost of Discipleship

66 In the course of research for *Loving God,* I discovered a dearth of contemporary writings on sin. After a long search, however, an unlikely source—Mike Wallace of "60 Minutes"—furnished just what I was looking for.

Since Christians are not accustomed to gleaning theological insights from network TV, I'd better explain.

Introducing a recent story about Nazi Adolf Eichmann, a principal architect of the Holocaust, Wallace posed a central question at the program's outset: "How is it possible . . . for a man to act as Eichmann acted? . . . Was he a monster? A madman? Or was he perhaps something even more terrifying: was he normal?"

Normal? The executioner of millions of Jews *normal?* Most self-respecting viewers would be outraged at the very thought.

The most startling answer to Wallace's shocking question came in an interview with Yehiel Dinur, a concentration camp survivor who testified against Eichmann at the Nuremburg trials. A film clip from Eichmann's 1961 trial showed Dinur walking into the courtroom, stopping short, seeing Eichmann for the first time since the Nazi had sent him to Auschwitz eighteen years earlier. Dinur began to sob uncontrollably, then fainted, collapsing in a heap on the floor as the presiding judicial officer pounded his gavel for order in the crowded courtroom.

Was Dinur overcome by hatred? Fear? Horrid memories?

No; it was none of these. Rather, as Dinur explained to Wallace, all at once he realized Eichmann was not the godlike army officer who had sent so many to their deaths. This Eichmann was an ordinary man. "I was afraid about myself," said Dinur. " . . . I saw that I am capable to do this. *I am . . . exactly*

41

like he."

Wallace's subsequent summation of Dinur's terrible discovery—"Eichmann is in all of us"—is a horrifying statement; but it indeed captures the central truth about man's nature. For as a result of the Fall, *sin is in each of us*—not just the susceptibility to sin, but sin itself.

The 3,500 years of recorded history confirm this truth. Science, evolution and education—which Socrates argued would eliminate sin—have done nothing to alter man's moral nature. Only the gospel of Jesus Christ can change our hearts. But we can't see that truth unless we first see our hearts as they really are.

That being so, why is sin so seldom written or preached about? Dinur's dramatic collapse in the Nuremburg courtroom gives us the clue. For to truly confront evil—the sin within us— is a devastating experience.

If the reality of man's sin was forthrightly preached, it would have the same shattering effect on blissful churchgoers that it had on Dinur. Many would flee their pews never to return. And since church growth is today's supreme standard of spirituality, many pastors steer away from such confrontative subjects; so do authors who want their books bought and read. So do television preachers whose success depends on audience ratings; for viewers confronted with hard truth can simply flick the offending preacher out of their living rooms.

The result is that the message is often watered down to a palatable gospel of positive thinking which will "hold the audience." That's what Nazi victim Dietrich Bonhoeffer called "cheap grace"—that in which "no contrition is required, still less any real desire to be delivered from sin."

But it's the very heart of a Christian conversion to confront one's own sin and thus to desperately desire deliverance from it. And once we've seen our sin, we can only live in gratitude for God's amazing grace. I know this most intimately from personal experience.

During the throes of Watergate, I went to talk with my friend Tom Phillips. I was curious, maybe even a little envious, about the changes in his life. His explanation—that he had "accepted Jesus Christ"—baffled me. I was tired, empty inside, sick of scandal and accusations, but not once did I see myself as having really sinned. Politics was a dirty business, and I was good at it. And what I had done, I rationalized, was no different from the usual political maneuvering. What's more, right and wrong were relative, and my motives were for the good of the country—or so I believed.

But that night when I left Tom's home and sat alone at my car, my own sin—not just dirty politics, but the hatred and pride and evil so deep within me—was thrust before my eyes, forcefully and painfully. For the first time in my life, I felt unclean, and worst of all, I could not escape. In those moments of clarity I found myself driven irresistibly into the arms of the living God.

And in the years since that night, I've grown increasingly aware of my own sinful nature; what is good in me I know beyond all doubt comes only through the righteousness of Jesus Christ. And for that *fact,* my gratitude to God deepens with each passing day, a gratitude that can only be expressed in His service.

Dinur, the Auschwitz survivor, is right—Eichmann is in us, each of us. But until we can face that truth, dreadful as it may be, cheap grace and lukewarm faith—the hallmarks of ungrateful hearts—will continue to abound in a crippled church.

Who Speaks for God?

Opening Reflection
1.   a. How would you answer Mike Wallace's question, "Was Adolf Eichmann normal?"

b. Can you say with Yehiel Dinur, "I am exactly like he"? Explain your response.

2. Do you agree that the reality of sin and the need for repentance is not clearly preached in churches and on TV? Why or why not?

3. Discuss the following statement: "Eichmann is in us, each of us. But until we can face that truth, dreadful as it may be, cheap grace and lukewarm faith—the hallmarks of ungrateful hearts— will continue to abound in a crippled church."

Turning to the Scriptures
4. Read Romans 3:9-20.

   a. What does this passage say about all human beings?

   b. Since all are sinners, what provision has God made for our salvation?

5. Study Jesus' dialogue with Nicodemus in John 3:1-21.

   a. How does one enter the Kingdom of God? (See especially verses 3 and 6.)

   b. Briefly describe your own experience with the new birth.

6.   a. What is the proper response to the coming of God's
      Kingdom, according to Mark 1:15?

      b. Based on Acts 26:20, how do we demonstrate that we have
      indeed repented?

7. Read Matthew 16:24-28. How does Jesus describe the cost of
being His follower?

8.   a. In Matthew 8:18-22, we read of two men who were unwill-
      ing to commit to following Jesus fully. What held each one
      back?

      b. What prevents you from following Jesus with greater
      commitment?

9. In Romans 7:14-25, Paul declared, "I have the desire to do what is good, but I cannot carry it out. For what I do is not the good I want to do; no, the evil I do not want to do—this I keep on doing" (verses 18-19).

a. How does your own experience of the Christian life compare with Paul's?

b. What does this experience say about our need for repentance?

10. What truths in Romans 8:1-14 provide the answer to the Christian's ongoing struggle against sin in his or her life?

11. Read Jesus' parable in Luke 18:9-14.

    a. Do you identify more with the Pharisee or with the tax collector?

    b. Why did the tax collector go home justified rather than the Pharisee?

12. Read 2 Samuel 12:1-14.

    a. What sin had David committed?

    b. Why do you think David could more easily see the sin of the man in Nathan's story than his own sin?

    c. What applications are there in this passage for recognizing sin in one's life?

13. Complex political issues are sometimes reduced to simplistic terms such as "good guys" and "bad guys" or "righteous nations" versus "evil empires." How do some of the insights gained in this session help correct this tendency?

14. List any questions you have at this point in your study.

For Further Reflection

The real battle is being fought . . . not between "good" people and "bad" people, like a game of cops and robbers; it is not between "good" governments and "bad," like the U.S. and the Soviet Union. It is not being fought for mere national or international stakes. The war to end all wars is a battle for eternal stakes between spiritual forces—and it is being waged in you and in me.

When we truly smell the stench of sin within us, it drives us helplessly and irresistibly to despair. But God *has provided a way for us to be freed from the evil within: it is through the door of repentance. When we truly comprehend our own nature, repentance is no dry doctrine, no frightening message, no morbid form of self-flagellation. It is, as the early church fathers said, a gift God grants which leads to life. It is the key to the door of liberation, to the only real freedom we can ever know.*

Charles Colson,
Loving God

The Greek word for repentance found in the New Testament is metanoia: meta, *meaning change, and* noia, *meaning mind. Repentance, as Christ preached it, is a changing of the mind, the intellect, the values. That inevitably produces a profound change of the heart and emotions, a total radical transformation from seeking to please self to seeking to please God. Repentance leads to nothing less than a human revolution. . . .*

Repentance is demanded not only for our individual sins, but for the sins for which we inescapably share responsibility as well. We are part and parcel of the society in which we live and the church we belong to. One of my favorite Old Testament figures is Nehemiah. He clearly understood the need to repent for himself and for the sins of his people. Before undertaking the seemingly impossible task of bringing the exiled Jews back to Jerusalem and rebuilding its walls, Nehemiah confessed "the sins of the sons of Israel which we have sinned against thee; I and my father's house have sinned." A repentant Nehemiah was greatly used by God; revival followed in the land.

Charles Colson,
Who Speaks for God?

When Jesus said to his disciples "how hard it is to enter the Kingdom of God, " it seems to have been natural for them to respond with the question, "who then can be saved?" (Mark 10:24-26).

Once this identification has been made, salvation takes on a broader aspect. For the Kingdom of God is God's dynamic rule, breaking into human history through Jesus, confronting, combatting, and overcoming evil, spreading the wholeness of personal and communal wellbeing, taking possession of his people in total blessing and total demand. The church is meant to be the Kingdom community, a model of what human community looks like when it comes under the

*rule of God, and a challenging alternative to secular society. Enter-
ing God's Kingdom is entering the new age, long promised in the Old
Testament, which is also the beginning of God's new creation. Now
we look forward to the consummation of the Kingdom when our
bodies, our society, and our universe will all be renewed, and sin,
pain, futility, disease, and death will all be eradicated. Salvation is
a big concept; we have no liberty to reduce it.*

John Stott,
*Involvement: Being a Responsible Christian
in a Non-Christian Society*

*The first of Luther's 95 theses nailed to the Wittenburg door was,
you recall, simply this, "When our Lord and Master Jesus Christ
said repent, He willed that the entire life of believers be one of
repentance."*

*The Christian needs the church to be a repenting community.
The Christian needs the church to be a zone of truth in a world of
mendacity, to be a community in which our sin need not be disguised,
but can be honestly faced and plainly confessed because we know that
the worst word about us as sinners is not the last word. The last word
is about us as sinners forgiven.*

*Through the shed blood of Jesus Christ our Lord we are embold-
ened to let the church be the church, a community resounding with
the no and yes of God's thunderous judgment and immeasurable
mercy. This is the Living Word that shatters our human pretensions
and conceits and then, after the shattering, tenderly picks up the
broken pieces of our lives and fits them together in the likeness of Him
Who makes all things new.*

Richard J. Neuhaus,
"The Christian and the Church"

*We will never find answers to our problems, at home or abroad, until
we face the truth about the human condition. Yet our very nature
makes us invariably look for evil everywhere except the one place
we're sure to find it. And sadly the church all too often fails to
preach the convicting truth.*

*America's blend of civil religion, humanism and comforting
platitudes may be good politics—but good politics can make bad
theology. Ironically, one of the most discerning voices of our times is
a former prisoner of the "evil empire" President Reagan spoke*

about. Following his conversion to Christ in the Soviet gulag, Aleksandr Solzhenitsyn wrote, ". . . it was disclosed to me that the line separating good and evil passes not through states, nor between classes, nor between parties either—but right through every human heart—through all human hearts."

The evil empire? We needn't search distant continents. The Bible tells us where to look. It is in us.

Charles Colson,
Who Speaks for God?

Moving into Action

Begin by having group members report on the action steps they have taken. If anyone has brought articles to share, take time for brief summaries.

Let group members choose from among these action steps.

1. Research the life and writings of Aleksandr Solzhenitsyn and report back to your group.

2. Read one of the books in the "Reading Resources" section and prepare a summary.

3. Continue to watch for articles on the relationship between the Christian faith and politics.

4. Report on the life of Dietrich Bonhoeffer, Christian martyr during the Nazi era.

5. Choose an issue—whether local, national, or international—of particular concern to you. Discuss with the group what actions you might take to get involved.

6. Pray individually about what God is calling you to do in the way of discipleship.

Ideas for Group Worship

Have a group member lead the group in a prayer of commitment to Christ and His Kingdom. Ask God to remove any barriers that prevent you from truly repenting and following Christ as Lord. Continue to pray about issues of special concern to your group.

Reading Resources

Dietrich Bonhoeffer, *The Cost of Discipleship* (New York: Macmillan, 1963).

Jerry Bridges, *The Pursuit of Holiness* (Colorado Springs, Colo.: NavPress, 1978).

Charles Colson, *Who Speaks for God?* (Westchester, Ill.: Cross-way Books, 1985).

Sinclair Ferguson, *Kingdom Life in a Fallen World* (Colorado Springs, Colo.: NavPress, 1986).

Jerry White, *Choosing Plan A in a Plan B World* (Colorado Springs, Colo.: NavPress, 1987).

Dual Citizenship

"After a recent lecture on a college campus I was asked, "Mr. Colson, how can you try to live by the Sermon on the Mount and at the same time support the use of military might?"

It's a fair question. Jesus teaches that we should love our enemies, return good for evil. But is this realistic in a world in which evil so often triumphs? Can one forgive seventy times seven and still restrain wrongdoers? Turn the other cheek to terrorism?

These dilemmas lead many to conclude that either Jesus was not speaking literally or if He was, one must live a monastic life to be a Christian. We reach such conclusions, however, because we misunderstand Jesus' teaching about the Kingdom.

When Jesus announced the Kingdom, He did indeed set forth radical standards by which its citizens are to live. He knew such a lifestyle would be both costly and complex, but it would witness the values of God's Kingdom even in the midst of the evil of this world. Christ was not suggesting, however, that the obedient Christian would be able to usher in the Kingdom of God on earth. Only Christ Himself would do that when He returns.

But for this period between the two stages—the announcement of the Kingdom and its final consummation—God has provided structures to restrain the evil of this world. The state is even ordained to wield the sword when necessary; and the Christian is commanded to obey the state and to respect its authority as God's instrument.

The Christian, therefore, follows two commandments: to live by Christ's teaching in the Sermon on the Mount, modeling the values of God's Kingdom—*the one yet to come in its*

55

fullness—and at the same time to support government's role in preserving order as a witness to God's authority over the present kingdoms of this world. So while the Christian is not to return evil for evil (he must instead exercise forgiveness, breaking the cycle of evil), he may participate in the God-ordained structure that restrains the evil and chaos of the fallen world by the use of force. . . .

The *state* was instituted by God to restrain sin and promote a just social order. One of the most common misconceptions in Western political thought is that the role of government is determined solely by the will of the people. When Pilate questioned Jesus on the eve of His execution, Christ told the governor that he would not even hold his office or political authority if it had not been granted him by God. The apostle Paul spoke of civil authority as "God's servant, an agent of wrath to bring punishment on the wrongdoer." Peter used similar language, saying that governments were set by God to "punish those who do wrong and to commend those who do right."

Government originated as an ordinance of God. It is, in one sense, God's response to the nature of the people themselves. Man "can adapt himself somehow to anything his imagination can cope with . . . but he cannot deal with chaos." While it cannot redeem the world or be used as a tool to establish the Kingdom of God, civil government does set the boundaries for human behavior. The state is not a remedy for sin, but a means to restrain it. Its limited task is to promote "the good of the community in temporal concerns, the protection of life and property and the preservation of peace and order."

When God established ancient Israel as a nation, His first order of business was the propagation of law, not just for religious purposes, but for the ordering of civil life. Even before the giving of the Ten Commandments there was great need for civil adjudication.

The biblical text records that "Moses took his seat to serve as judge for the people and they stood around him from morning till evening." (Court dockets seemed to have been clogged from the very beginning.) Moses explained that "the people come to me to seek God's will. Whenever they have a dispute, it is brought to me, and I decide between the parties and inform them of God's decrees and laws."

Thus the Israelite involved in a dispute looked not to the whim of a judge or to an arbitrary law but rather to a ruling based on divine laws. The judicial role was not a mechanism to advance the state's perception of social equilibrium, but to discern God's revealed law.

This is the origin of what we call the rule of law; it stands in stark contrast to modern moral relativism. Without transcendent norms, laws are either established by social elites or are merely bargains struck by competing forces in society. In the Judeo-Christian view, law is rooted in moral absolutes that do not vacillate with public taste or the whim of fashion.

Thus rooted, government can perform not only the negative function of restraining evil, but the positive function of promoting a just social order so that people can live in harmony. The apostle Paul had this in mind when he urged his young colleague Timothy to pray "for kings and all those in authority, that we may live peaceful and quiet lives in all godliness and holiness."

In the words of sociologist Robert Nisbet, man is engaged in a continual "quest for community." It is important to remember, however, that the state is not itself that community. Anyone who has ever dealt with a government bureaucracy knows that it is rare enough to get a phone call through, let alone to cultivate warm fuzzy feelings for the mammoth machine of big government.

But the state can protect people's voluntary efforts to shape community by granting equal protection of the law, by upholding principles of justice so the weak and powerless are not exploited, and by guaranteeing liberty and providing security. In this way the government sustains a stable environment in which people can live, producing art, literature, music, and children. Or as C. S. Lewis alluded to it, they can partake of one of the primary benefits of democracy: the simple freedom to enjoy a cup of tea by the fire with one's family.

Christianity teaches, then, that the state serves a divinely appointed and divinely defined task, although it is not in itself divine. Its authority is legitimate, though limited.

Kingdoms in Conflict

Opening Reflection

1. "The state was instituted by God to restrain sin and promote a just social order."

    a. In what sense does government restrain or attempt to restrain sin?

    b. What is your understanding of "a just social order"?

    c. In what ways—both real and ideal—does government function to achieve this goal of justice?

2. What are the limitations of government in providing an environment for human existence? What can it *not* do?

3. How does the Judeo-Christian understanding of law differ from that of modern relativism?

Turning to the Scriptures
4. Read Romans 13:1-7.

a. What does this passage say about the origin of the governing authorities?

b. What, therefore, are Christians urged to do?

c. What is a ruler (or government official) called in verse 4?

d. How does this identity give him authority?

e. In what way does it also limit his authority?

f. What do we owe government, according to verse 7?

5. Study 1 Peter 2:13-17.

a. According to Peter, what is the function of government (verse 14)?

b. What should be the Christian's basic stance toward government?

c. What should be the result of our submission to government? (See especially verses 16-17.)

6. In Jesus' trial before Pilate (John 19:1-16), Pilate reminded Jesus of his power as a Roman governor. What did Jesus say about Pilate's power?

7. As we have seen, Scripture clearly teaches that government is the servant of God.

   a. What happens when government forgets or rejects this role?

   b. What is the Christian's responsibility in a situation like that?

8. Read Acts 4:1-21.

   a. What command had the Jewish authorities given the apostles?

   b. How did the apostles justify their disobedience to authority?

9. Use your study of the passages from Acts, Romans, and 1 Peter (questions 4, 5, and 8 of this session) to answer the following three questions.

a. Under what conditions do you believe Christians are justified, or obligated, to disobey government?

b. If you believe that "civil disobedience" is sometimes legitimate, what forms might it properly take?

c. Do you believe that a Christian could ever justly participate in a revolution against government? Why or why not?

10. In Matthew 10:37, Jesus said, "Anyone who loves his father or mother more than me is not worthy of me; anyone who loves his son or daughter more than me is not worthy of me." How might this principle also apply to our relationship to government?

11. The Christian is a citizen of a political nation, such as the United States, and also a citizen of the Kingdom of God.

    a. In what ways can a Christian be a good patriot?

    b. What are the limitations on the Christian's patriotism?

12. How would you summarize the Christian's responsibility toward government?

13. List any questions or comments you have at this point.

For Further Reflection

The Kingdom of God . . . is not a blueprint for some new social order; nor does it merely set the forces of radical cultural change in motion. Rather, God's Kingdom promises radical changes in human personalities.

This is the crucial point. While human politics is based on the premise that society must be changed in order to change people, in the politics of the Kingdom it is people who must be changed in order to change society.

Through men and women who recognize its authority and live by its ethical standards, the Kingdom of God invades the stream of history. It breaks the vicious and otherwise irreversible cycles of violence, injustice, and self-interest. In this way the Kingdom of God equips its citizens, as Augustine said, to be the best citizens in the kingdom of man.

Charles Colson,
Kingdoms in Conflict

When the church dares to be different, it models for the world what God calls the world to become. The church models what it means to be a community of caring and a community of character. For us Christians, what we can do is more limited and finally less interesting and important than what by the grace of God we can be. We have no illusions, or we ought to have no illusions, about our ability to establish the Kingdom of God on earth. We do indeed strive to build a world in which the strong are just, and power is tempered by mercy, in which the weak are nurtured and those at the entrance gates and those at the exit gates of life are protected both by law and love. We strive for such a society—not because success is guaranteed, but because love for the neighbor is commanded. And yet we know that short of the coming of the Kingdom of God, the principalities and powers of the present age will rage. And in the eyes of the world, and sometimes in our own eyes, they will make a mockery of all our striving to transform the world. And yet, again, we persist in striving, driven not by illusions of success, but empowered by a promise. And the promise is that in the final accounting nothing done for the love of Christ is done in vain. And through our disappointments and through our mistakes and in our weariness, defying the appearance of futility comes the word of our Master, "Fear not, little flock, it is my Father's good pleasure to give you the kingdom."

We will not succeed in building the society that we desire. But the church can more fully be that society—the society it is our destiny and our duty to be. The world needs the church to be the church.

Richard J. Neuhaus,
"The Christian and the Church"

A Chinese residing in France thinks in his own terms, in his own tradition; he has his own criterion of judgment and of action; he is really a stranger and a foreigner: he is also a citizen of another State, and his loyalty is given to this State, and not to the country in which he is living. It is the same with the Christian; he is the citizen of another Kingdom, and it is thence that he derives his way of thinking, judging, and feeling. His heart and his thought are elsewhere. He is the subject of another State, he is the ambassador of this State upon earth; that is to say, he ought to present the demands of his Master, he establishes a relation between the two, but he cannot take the side of this world. He stands up for the interests of his Master, as an ambassador champions the interests of his country. From another point of view (and here the relation is quite different), he may also be sent out as a spy. In fact, that may be the situation of the Christian: to work in secret, at the heart of the world, for his Lord; to prepare for the Lord's victory from within; to create a nucleus in this world, and to discover its secrets, in order that the Kingdom of God may break forth in splendour.

Jacques Ellul,
The Presence of the Kingdom

With the emergence of a monolithic state that seeks all power for itself, the church is called to rethink the implications of Romans 13 where Paul commands respect and honor for the state. But in inter-

preting these passages, we must not confuse the state with the nation. Government as such should always be given respect by the community of the faithful, for otherwise society could fall into anarchy. But respect for government should not be confused with veneration of the nation or people (das Volk) *who represent a particular cultural and ethnic heritage. Nationalism and racism are modern idolatries, and when the state is made to serve the aspirations of race or nation instead of the cause of justice for all, it becomes a demonic state warranting resistance and rejection by the Christian faithful (cf. Revelation 13).*

Donald Bloesch,
Crumbling Foundations

Contemporary appeals to Romans 13 often fail to realize the implications of Paul's teaching for contemporary democratic *societies. On the most conservative reading of this passage, as applied to Paul's audience, the Apostle was insisting that the authority and mandate to govern, even in totalitarian societies, are given to human beings by God, so that one may not lightly dismiss the obligation to respect and obey political powers. But in modern democracies the power of national leaders is derived from the populace, which is the* primary *locus of God-given authority. Built into the very process is the possibility of review, debate, reexamination, election, and defeat. Given such a framework, for Christians simply to acquiesce in a present policy is to* fail to respect *the governing authorities—in the primary sense, as understood in democratic theory. Democratic government grants Christians the right publicly to criticize, review, debate, and challenge current procedures and policies. Under those conditions, the message of Romans 13 imposes on them the duty to make use of that right.*

Richard J. Mouw,
Political Evangelism

Moving into Action

Begin by having group members report on the action steps they have taken. If anyone has brought articles to share, take time for brief summaries.

Choose from among the following action steps.

1. Do further study on the issue of civil disobedience. Several members may wish to undertake this study as a team.

2. Follow up on the specific issue you may have identified to get involved with by sharing with the group action steps you have taken or are planning to take.

3. Prepare a summary for the group on how Christian faith relates to a particular political situation.

Ideas for Group Worship

Sing a hymn like "I Love Thy Kingdom, Lord" or "O Worship the King."

Thank God for the gift of government. Pray for local, national, and international leaders. Your group might want to select a few of these men and women by name to pray for regularly during your remaining sessions.

Continue to pray about needs identified in the newspaper and magazine articles.

Reading Resources

Charles Colson, *Kingdoms in Conflict* (New York/Grand Rapids: William Morrow/Zondervan Publishing House, 1987).

Charles Colson, *The Role of The Church in Society* (Wheaton, Ill.: Victor Books, 1986).

J. Marcellus Kik, *The Story of Two Kingdoms* (New York: Nelson, 1963).

Stephen Charles Mott, *Biblical Ethics and Social Change* (New York: Oxford University Press, 1982).

Richard J. Mouw, *Political Evangelism* (Grand Rapids: Eerdmans Publishing Co., 1973).

Richard John Neuhaus, *The Naked Public Square: Religion and Democracy in America* (Grand Rapids: Eerdmans Publishing Co., 1984).

Arthur Simon, *Christian Faith and Public Policy: No Grounds for Divorce* (Grand Rapids: Eerdmans Publishing Co., 1987).

The Christian and Politics

*Frequently I'm asked whether I would have partici-
pated in Watergate if I had been a Christian when I
worked in the White House. The implication is that
Christians are immune to corruption.*

I'm always tempted to say, "Of course not." But that's self-
righteous nonsense. While Christians know that their faith
requires high standards of righteousness, they are human and
often capitulate to the same temptations as anyone else. In
fact, Christians may well face more problems than others
when they become involved in the political process.

How does a Christian deal with the inherent divided loyal-
ties: duty to God and duty to the national interest? Can a Christian successfully avoid the subtle snares of power? Can a
Christian make the compromises necessary for the everyday
business of politics?

What about the question of candor, for example? At times
national security may well require not only concealing the
truth, but lying. When I was in the White House, we went to
elaborate lengths to conceal essential secret negotiations.
Henry Kissinger had a bad cold when he visited Pakistan in
1971—or so we told the press. Actually he had been flown to
Bejing to conduct clandestine meetings in preparation for Mr.
Nixon's historic visit to China.

Or take the day Nixon announced a major troop with-
drawal in Vietnam. He immediately ordered Kissinger to bring
Soviet Ambassador Dobrynin to a secret meeting room in the
White House basement. "Henry," he roared, "You shake him
up. Tell him not to believe these news stories. We're only pull-
ing out a few troops—and if the Russians don't back off in
sending supplies to Hanoi, we'll bomb the daylights out of that
city. Tell him the president is uncontrollable, a madman—that

69

he'll do anything. Let's keep them off balance." That such meetings took place was flatly denied in order to protect the lives of the withdrawing troops.

President Reagan did the same thing in 1983. When reporters asked about a rumored invasion of Grenada, official White House spokesmen dismissed such questions as "preposterous." Actually, troops were at that moment disembarking on the island's beaches. A "no comment" to the press, however, would have been tantamount to a "yes"—an admission that would have endangered lives.

In these days of delicate international tensions and the instant communications ability of an almost omnipresent press, such deceit is a common instrument of foreign policy. The press even accept it. In a 1987 *Newsweek* interview, crack ABC interviewer Ted Koppel acknowledged that government officials must be "prepared to mislead and . . . sometimes even to lie."

Deliberate lies, the corruption of power, compromise with ideological opponents, temptations on all sides—these appear to be the mechanisms of modern government. Should the Christian circumvent the messy business of politics altogether?

The answer must be an emphatic no. As Robert L. Dabney wrote, "Every Christian . . . whether law-maker or law executor or voter, should carry his Christian conscience, enlightened by God's Word, into his political duty. We must ask less what party caucuses and leaders dictate, and more what duty dictates."

There are at least three compelling reasons Christians must be involved in politics and government. First, as citizens of the nation-state, Christians have the same civic duties all citizens have: to serve on juries, to pay taxes, to vote, to support candidates they think are best qualified. They are commanded to pray for and respect governing authorities. (For years many Christian fundamentalists shunned the "sinful" political process, even to the extent of not voting. Whatever else may be said about it, the Moral Majority performed a valuable public service in bringing these citizens back into the mainstream.)

Second, as citizens of the Kingdom of God they are to

bring God's standards of righteousness and justice to bear on the kingdoms of this world. This is the cultural commission discussed earlier. As former Michigan state senator and college professor Stephen Monsma says, Christian political involvement has the "potential to move the political system away from . . . the brokering of the self-interest of powerful persons and groups into a renewed concern for the public interest."

Third, Christians have an obligation to bring transcendent moral values into the public debate. All law implicitly involves morality; the popular idea that "you can't legislate morality" is a myth. Morality is legislated every day from the vantage point of one value system or another. The question is not whether we will legislate morality, but whose morality we will legislate.

Kingdoms in Conflict

Opening Reflection

1. Do you think there are any valid reasons for Christians to avoid involvement in the political process?

2. What to you are the most important reasons why Christians must be involved in government and politics?

3.   a. What has been your involvement in the political process (for example, voting, campaigning, attending party caucuses, writing to legislators, running for public office)?

   b. How do you feel about your level of involvement?

4. "Christians may well face more problems than others when they become involved in the political process." Do you agree? Why or why not?

Turning to the Scriptures
5. Read 1 Timothy 2:1-7.

   a. For whom are we especially urged to pray?

   b. What is the goal of such prayer?

c. Do you have a regular or systematic way of praying for those in government? If not, how might that be done?

6. God's prophets in the Old Testament had much to say about politics and government. What light do the following passages shed on the kind of people we should elect to public office?

Isaiah 3:13-15

Isaiah 10:1-4

Jeremiah 22:1-5

7. Psalm 72 describes an ideal king.

a. Summarize this description.

b. What traits would also be desirable in an elected public official in a democracy?

8. a. When you vote, how much do you take into consideration a candidate's religious position?

b. How important do you think this position is in a candidate's desirability or appropriateness for public office?

9. a. In addition to informed voting, what other channels are available to a Christian for having an impact on political issues?

b. Which of these channels have you used? (If you have used several, describe which have been most satisfactory and least satisfactory.)

10. Study the encounter between Jesus and the Pharisees in Matthew 22:15-22.

a. Under what circumstances did Jesus make the statement about Caesar and God?

b. What do you believe you owe to Caesar (government)?

c. What do you owe to God?

11. Read 1 Kings 21:1-28.

a. What wrong had King Ahab done?

b. How did God's prophet confront him?

c. Do you think the church has a responsibility today to publicly expose any government immorality? Why or why not?

12. a. How do you understand the concept of separation of church and state?

b. Based on your study so far, what biblical support can you point to for this policy?

13. Can Christians be vigorous advocates for justice and morality without destroying the separation of church and state? (If no, why not? If yes, what ways are most effective and appropriate?)

14. In the light of your study so far, evaluate the following statements.

    a. "Religion and politics don't mix."

    b. "You can't legislate morality."

15. List any questions or comments you have.

For Further Reflection

The words "politics" and "political" may be given either a broad or a narrow definition. Broadly speaking, "politics" denotes the life of the city (polis) and the responsibilities of the citizen (polites). It is concerned therefore with the whole of our life in human society. Politics is the art of living together in community. According to its narrow definition, however, politics is the science of government. It is concerned with the development and adoption of specific policies with a view to their being enshrined in legislation.

    Once this distinction is clear, we may ask whether Jesus was involved in politics. In the latter and narrow sense, he clearly was

*not. He never formed a political party, adopted a political pro-
gramme or organised a political protest. He took no steps to influence
the policies of Caesar, Pilate, or Herod. On the contrary, he
renounced a political career. In the other and broader sense of the
word, however, his whole ministry was political. For he had himself
come into the world, in order to share in the life of the human community, and he sent his followers into the world to do the same.
Moreover, the Kingdom of God he proclaimed and inaugurated was
a radically new and different social organisation, whose values and
standards challenged those of the old and fallen community. In this
way his teaching had "political" implications. It offered an alternative to the status quo. His kingship, moreover, was perceived as a
challenge to Caesar's, and he was therefore accused of sedition.*

John Stott,
*Involvement: Being a Responsible Christian
in a Non-Christian Society*

*Let me suggest a fundamental distinction, one that undergirds my
thinking: the distinction between the separation of church and state
on the one hand, and the separation of religion and life on the other
hand. The separation of church and state, properly understood, is a
principle of fundamental importance to the nation. The separation of
religion from life is pure heresy. It is false because it contradicts the
biblical witness and therefore the Christian understanding of faith.
To take major areas of life, those having to do with social and eco-
nomic decisions that vitally affect all of us, and put them in a com-
partment carefully separated from faith is to turn much of life over
to the devil. It is another way of making Christianity into a one-
hour-on-Sunday religion, or perhaps a faith that has nothing to do
with one's business or professional career and certainly not—God
forbid!—with politics. This view is heresy because it locks God out of
much of life. It is the opposite of confessing Jesus as Lord.*

Arthur Simon,
*Christian Faith and Public Policy:
No Grounds for Divorce*

*Tension between church and state is inherent and inevitable. Indeed,
it is perhaps the outworking of one of God's great mysteries, part of
the dynamic by which He governs His universe. For from the constant tension—the chafing back and forth—a certain equilibrium*

is achieved.

To maintain the balance the church and the state must fulfill their respective roles. One cannot survive without the other, yet neither can do the work of the other. Both operate under God's rule, each in a different relationship to that rule.

Certainly one thing is clear. When they fail in their appointed tasks—that is, when the church fails to be the visible manifestation of the Kingdom of God and the state fails to maintain justice and concord—civic order collapses.

Charles Colson,
Kingdoms in Conflict

Politics is not the church's first calling. Evangelism, administering the sacraments, providing discipleship, fellowship, teaching the Word, and exhorting its members to holy living are the heartbeat of the church. When it addresses political issues, the church must not do so at the risk of weakening its primary mission. As mainline churches discovered in the sixties, the faster they churned out partisan state-ments, the faster they emptied the pews.

Charles Colson,
Kingdoms in Conflict

There is not a Christian attitude which can be applied to all times, but according to different times, attitudes which appear to be contra-dictory, may be equally good, to the extent in which they make their mark on history as fidelity to the purpose of God. Thus it is not necessary to be loyal to an idea, to a doctrine, or to a political move-ment. What is called "fidelity" in the language of the world is too often only habit or obstinacy. The Christian may belong to the Right or to the Left, he may be a Liberal or a Socialist, according to the times in which he lives, and according as the position of the one or the other seems to him more in harmony with the will of God at that par-ticular time. These attitudes are contradictory, it is true, from the human point of view, but their unity consists in the search for the coming Kingdom.

Jacques Ellul,
The Presence of the Kingdom

For many people, the concept of separation of church and state has come to mean the separation of state and God, as if the state ruled autonomously on the basis of its own intrinsic authority. Christians must never believe that. Instead, we must see that state as answerable to God, ordained by God, and as a legitimate vehicle for the people of God to serve God.

It is certainly legitimate, and in some cases desirable, for Christians to be actively involved in the political process. I see no reason why a Christian should not or could not run for state office and serve Christ by being a godly ruler. However, it becomes increasingly difficult for a Christian to get elected, playing the "games" that are often demanded of that person, without compromising his integrity. That is the razor's edge that a would-be Christian politician has to walk. It is still possible in this country to be elected to high office without compromising one's personal integrity. It may be difficult, but it is still possible.

R.C. Sproul,
*Life Views: Understanding the Ideas
That Shape Society Today*

It is one thing for an individual Christian to address whatever issue his or her conscience dictates, but the church as a body, which purports to speak God's truth, should speak only to those matters in which fidelity to holy Scripture itself makes it necessary to speak out: issues where human life or dignity, religious liberty, or justice are involved. Even then, the church should claim no superior wisdom except in those areas where they are uniquely able to bring biblically informed truth to the debate.

Charles Colson,
Kingdoms in Conflict

Moving into Action

Have group members report on the action steps they have taken. Take time to hear brief summaries of any newspaper or magazine articles that were brought in.

Choose from among the following activities.

1. Explain how to write to elected officials on issues of concern. Locate the names and addresses of local, state, and national legislators and executives.

2. Invite a Christian active in a political party to speak to your group about the opportunities and problems of Christians in politics. Or, interview a Christian in politics and share your

findings with your group.

3. Research the history of the separation of church and state in our country.

4. Interview a superintendent of schools or a principal to learn how the issue of religious activities in the public schools is handled.

5. Continue to gather articles on issues relating to Christians in politics.

6. Pursue a course of action that you and the group have identified for your particular issue of concern.

Ideas for Group Worship
Let each group member who feels comfortable doing so pray a brief prayer for those in government, for Christians in politics, for issues in the news, or for your group and its study. Be sure to support each other in prayer for any action steps taken on specific issues.

Reading Resources
Charles Colson, *Kingdoms in Conflict* (New York/Grand Rapids: William Morrow/Zondervan Publishing House, 1987).

Charles Colson, *The Role of The Church in Society* (Wheaton, Ill.: Victor Books, 1986).

Stephen Charles Mott, *Biblical Ethics and Social Change* (New York: Oxford University Press, 1982).

Richard J. Mouw, *Political Evangelism* (Grand Rapids: Eerdmans Publishing Co., 1973).

Richard John Neuhaus, *The Naked Public Square: Religion and Democracy in America* (Grand Rapids: Eerdmans Publishing Co., 1984).

A. James Reichley, *Religion in American Public Life* (Washington, D.C.: Brookings Institute, 1985).

Arthur Simon, *Christian Faith and Public Policy: No Grounds for Divorce* (Grand Rapids: Eerdmans Publishing Co., 1987).

The Paradox of Power

In the process of announcing the Kingdom and offering redemption from the Fall, Jesus Christ turned conventional views of power upside down. When His disciples argued over who was the greatest, Jesus rebuked them. "The greatest among you should be like the youngest, and the one who rules like the one who serves," He said. Imagine the impact His statement would make in the back rooms of American politicians or in the carpeted boardrooms of big business—or, sadly, in some religious councils.

Jesus was as good as His words. He washed His own followers' dusty feet, a chore reserved for the lowliest servant of first-century Palestine. A king serving the mundane physical needs of His subjects? Incomprehensible. Yet servant leadership is the heart of Christ's teaching. "Whoever wants to be first must be slave of all."

His was a revolutionary message to the class-conscious culture of the first-century, where position and privilege were entrenched, evidenced by the Pharisees with their reserved seats in the synagogue, by masters ruling slaves, and by men dominating women. It is no less revolutionary today in the class-conscious cultures of the East and West where power, money, fame, and influence are idolized in various forms.

The Christian understanding of power is that it is found most often in weakness. This paradox has been a thorn in the flesh of tyrants. The Judeo-Christian teaching that man is vulnerable to the temptations of power has also caused democracies and free nations to build restraints and balances of power into their structures.

Clearly this is what motivated the revolutionaries in England to guarantee a Parliament independent of the monarchy.

And in America the Founding Fathers, influenced by Judeo-Christian teaching about the vulnerability of man, wisely adopted the principle of the separation of powers. Within the government, power was diffused through a system of checks and balances so no one branch could dominate another. The Founders also assumed that the religious value system, evidenced through the separate institution of the church, would be the most powerful brake on the natural avarice of government. As Tocqueville observed, "Religion in America takes no direct part in the government or society but it must, nevertheless, be regarded as the foremost of the political institutions of that country."

The most important restraint on power, however, is a healthy understanding of its true source. When power in the conventional sense is relinquished, one discovers a much deeper power.

Prisoners often discover this, as did Jerry Levin and Aleksandr Solzhenitsyn. In his memoirs of the gulag, Solzhenitsyn wrote that as long as he was trying to maintain some pitiful degree of worldly power in his situation—control of food, clothing, schedule—he was constantly under the heel of his captors. But after his conversion, when he accepted and surrendered to his utter powerlessness, then he became free of even his captors' power. Perhaps this is why Boris Pasternak once wrote that the only place one can be free in a communist society is in prison.

The apostle Paul said, "My power is made perfect in weakness," and concluded, "When I am weak, then I am strong." And throughout Scripture God reveals a special compassion for the powerless: widows, orphans, prisoners, and aliens. Though the message of the Kingdom of God offers salvation for all who repent and believe, God does not conceal His disdain for those so enamored of their own power that they refuse to worship Him or to acknowledge His delight in the humble.

A culture that exalts power and celebrity, that worships success, dismisses such words as nonsense. Strong individuals rely on their own resources—which will never, ultimately speaking, be enough—but the so-called weak person knows his or her own limits and needs, and thus depends wholly on

God. Perhaps this is why God so often confounds the wisdom of the world by accomplishing His purposes through the powerless and His most powerful work through human weakness.

I first learned this in prison. When the frustration of my helplessness seemed greatest, I discovered God's grace was more than sufficient. And after my imprisonment I could look back and see how God used my powerlessness for His purposes. What He has chosen for my most significant witness was not my triumphs or victories, but my defeat.

Similarly, Prison Fellowship's work in the prisons has been effective not because of any power we may have as an organization, but because of the powerlessness of those we serve. During an unforgettable trip to Peru in 1984, for example, I visited Lurigancho, the largest prison in the world. There seven thousand inmates, including a number of terrorists, were crowded in abysmal conditions; hatred, hostility, and despair seeped out of the cellblocks. Yet within the darkness of Lurigancho is a thriving Christian community—men who have found Christ and experienced renewed hearts and minds.

After visiting with these brothers, I went directly from the prison to meet with a number of government officials in downtown Lima. Covered with prison dust and marked with the sweaty embraces of Christian prisoners, I addressed these officials at the highest level of government—and they listened intently.

Had I gone to Peru specifically to meet with the key government leadership, I would have likely been stymied. They wanted to meet me not because of any power or influence I had, but because of our work in the prisons. They knew that in the chaos of Lurigancho, Prison Fellowship was doing something to bring healing and restoration. Therefore, they were eager to listen to our recommendations, ready to discuss a biblical view of justice and prison issues. Whatever authority I had in speaking to these powerful men came not from my power but from serving the powerless. I have experienced this in country after country. It is the paradox of real power.

Kingdoms in Conflict

Opening Reflection

1. How did Jesus turn conventional ideas of power upside down?

2. What signs do you see that our society "exalts power and celebrity" and "worships success"?

3. "When power in the conventional sense is relinquished, we discover a much deeper power." Do you really believe this is true? Why or why not?

Turning to the Scriptures

4. Read Mark 10:35-45. When James and John asked to sit at Jesus' right and left hand in glory, they were asking for positions of power.

a. How did Jesus correct their view of greatness in His Kingdom?

b. How is Jesus' teaching in contrast to the values of the kingdoms of this world?

c. How is Jesus our model in going against the grain of our culture?

5. Read the account of Jesus washing His disciples' feet, in John 13:1-17.

a. When in the course of Jesus' life did this significant event take place?

b. What truth was Jesus demonstrating?

c. What does it mean for you to be a servant . . .

in your home?

at church?

at work?

in your community?

in your nation?

in the world?

6. Read 2 Corinthians 12:7-10. What do you think Paul meant when he said, "When I am weak, then I am strong"?

7. Read John 18:28-40. Before Pilate, Jesus rejected the use of force in His Kingdom (verse 36).

    a. When is the use of force justified or unjustified in living by the values of God's Kingdom?

    b. Do you think it is right for Christians in a pluralistic society to impose a Christian lifestyle by law? Why or why not?

8. Read Jeremiah 29:4-9. Through His prophet Jeremiah, the Lord spoke these words to the people of Israel who were living as captives in Babylon. How might they also apply to our life in a society in which we are "outsiders"?

9.   a. What is the major teaching of Jesus' parable of the minas, or talents, as recorded in Luke 19:11-27?

b. How does this parable apply to us as we live as citizens of the Kingdom of God in the kingdoms of this world?

10. Read 1 Peter 2:9-12.

a. How does Peter identify Christians in this passage?

b. How might verse 12 apply to the political activities of Christians in a pluralistic society?

c. What are some agencies or organizations through which you can serve others in our society?

d. To what extent do you think Christians should team up with nonChristians to work on social concerns (for example: world hunger, criminal justice reform, pro-life issues, campaigns against drunk driving)?

11. a. List all the motives given in Colossians 1:9-14 for living "a life worthy of the Lord."

b. What are the implications of this passage for the Christian's involvement in his or her society?

12. List any questions or comments you have at the end of this session.

13. a. Are there any ways your thinking has been changed or
     expanded by this study?

     b. Have you taken any actions as a result? If so, describe
     them briefly.

c. Do you plan to make any changes in your life as a result of this study? If so, what are they?

For Further Reflection

If, in our vocation, we are able to serve the world by serving our fellowman in government, we are not acting against Christ. Quite the opposite is true. Government is an arena in which we as Christians are called to bear witness to the righteousness of Christ and to the style of government that Christ Himself exhibits. This does not mean that we take the church into the state. It does mean that we take Christians and their obedient life-style into government. The Christian lives in both spheres, church and state, and he has responsibilities to each.

R.C. Sproul,
*Life Views: Understanding the Ideas
That Shape Society Today*

Obedience is the beginning of the Christian life; obedience is essential to truly living as a Christian. But on every side today we are beset by temptations that carry us away from God. We live in the most materialistic, egocentric time in American history. It's hard to be an obedient Christian when our culture worships a false god of success. The world says, "Do your own thing"; the Gospel says, "Bear one another's burdens, and thus fulfill the law of Christ" (Galatians 6:2). The world says, "Look out for number one"; the Gospel says to "lay down our lives for the brethren" (1 John 3:16) and to "love your neighbor as yourself" (Mark 12:31). It takes courage to be obedient, courage found only in total dependence on the Holy Spirit.

Charles Colson,
The Role of the Church in Society

There is much to commend in voluntary assistance. But we also need to recognize its limitations—and its temptations. Voluntary aid (charity is still a good word for it) often brings with it the satisfaction of providing some measurable benefit to another. It is more concrete and more clearly grasped than the complexities of public policy. It is emotionally satisfying, as well as useful, to serve in a soup kitchen or to sponsor a child overseas. But the danger is that, feeling satisfied, we never ask why people are mired in hunger and poverty. What are the causes of their hunger? How can we do more than meet their immediate needs? How can we help to bring about changed conditions that will enable hungry people to become independent and contribute through their own skill and labor to a world less plagued by hunger?

Arthur Simon,
Christian Faith and Public Policy:
No Grounds for Divorce

God rules every aspect of what He has made. Life, death, relationships, and earthly kingdoms are all in His hands.

This totality of God's authority is a major reason many resent Christianity. They see it as an excuse for religious zealots to try to cram their absolute orders from their God down others' throats. And in doing so, they miss the central teaching of the Kingdom of God.

When Christ commanded His followers to "seek first the kingdom of God," He was exhorting them to seek to be ruled by God and gratefully acknowledge His power and authority over them. That means that the Christian's goal is not to strive to rule, but to be ruled.

While God's rule is authoritarian, it is also voluntary. The Good News is that the price has been paid, and His Kingdom is open for all who desire admission.

Charles Colson,
Kingdoms in Conflict

In recent years many Christians have urged a more direct approach for bringing needed social change: simply elect Christians to political office. One spokesman has even suggested a religious version of affirmative action; if, for example, 24 percent of the people are born again, then at least 24 percent of the officeholders should be born again. Others have argued that Christians should "take dominion" over government, with those in public office speaking "for God as well as for the American people."

On the surface, this shortcut might seem to some an appealing answer to America's declining morality. It is, however, simplistic and dangerous triumphalism. To suggest that electing Christians to public office will solve all public ills is not only presumptuous and theologically questionable, it is also untrue.

Today's misspent enthusiasm for political solutions to the moral problems of our culture arises from a distorted view of both politics and spirituality—too low a view of the power of a sovereign God and too high a view of the ability of man. The idea that human systems, reformed by Christian influence, pave the road to the Kingdom—or at least, to revival—has the same utopian ring that one finds in Marxist literature. It also ignores the consistent lesson of history that shows that laws are most often reformed as a result of powerful spiritual movements. I know of no case where a spiritual movement was achieved by passing laws.

Charles Colson,
Kingdoms in Conflict

Christians should be careful not to "baptise" any political ideology (whether of the right, the left or the centre) as if it contained a monopoly of truth and goodness. At best a political ideology and its programme are only an approximation to Christian or biblical ideas. The fact is that, at least in some parts of the world, Christians are to be found in virtually every political party and are able to defend their membership on conscientious Christian ground.

John Stott,
Involvement: Being a Responsible Christian
in a Non-Christian Society

Liberation theologians of a Marxist stripe on the left, and of a theonomist [reconstructionist] stripe on the right, would create a partisan church. Membership in a partisan church is defined, not by the gospel of God's justifying grace in Christ, but by ideology and political alignment and where you stand on the public policy issues of the day.

Indeed, in its extreme forms, ideology and politics are said to be the gospel of Jesus Christ. In its more tempered forms, this view has insinuated itself into our churches so that even Christians who think of themselves as moderate fall into the habit of mind by which they measure the church's mission by its influence on what is ridiculously called "the real world"—the world of political and social change. But moderate apostasy is still apostasy, and indeed it may be its more dangerous form for appearing so innocent, because its lethal implications are disguised by the appearance of moderation.

This apostasy means that, in many of our churches, God's people hunger for the Bread of Life and are too often given the stones borrowed from the deadly power games of the world. Preachers become influence peddlers, and churches are turned into political lobbies which, no matter how successful and how much clout they think they have, are in fact pitiful appendages to agendas that are set in the public arena by people who neither understand nor care about the nature and the mission of the church of Christ.

The church as a tool is a church of fools.

Richard J. Neuhaus,
"The Christian and the Church"

Wherever a political agenda is seen as constitutive of the Church, all those who dissent from it are excluded from the Church. In that very instant, the Church is no longer catholic; indeed, it ceases to be the Church.

Peter Berger,
"Different Gospels:
The Social Sources of Apostasy"

Power involves the use of coercive force to make others yield to one's wishes even against their own will. Authority is achieved—or is conferred upon one—by virtue of character that others are motivated to follow willingly.

Therefore, the citizen of the Kingdom should seek authority that comes from his or her own spiritual strength. Never for self-advantage, but for the benefit of others.

This does not mean that the Christian can't use power. In positions of leadership, especially in government institutions to which God has specifically granted the power of the sword, the Christian can do so in good conscience. But the Christian uses power with a

*different motive and in different ways: not to impose his or her per-
sonal will over others but to preserve God's plan for order and justice
for all.*

*Those who accept the biblical view of servant leadership treat
power as a humbling delegation from God, not as a right to control
others.*

Charles Colson,
Kingdoms in Conflict

Moving into Action

Have group members share the results of their action steps. Take
time to hear summaries of the clippings brought in. Choose from
among the following activities.

1. Prepare a list of local and national organizations through
which Christians can serve to bring the values of Christ's Kingdom into reality.

2. Find out what opportunities for service are available in
your own community.

3. Add to your collection of articles on Christian involvement in politics.

4. Formulate a long-range plan for continuing your involvement in an area of special concern to you.

Note: Your group will probably want to meet one more time
to hear reports on actions taken. You may also want to summarize what you have learned and decide whether there is some continuing involvement you wish to do as a group. Plan for some
closing worship time together. Your group may also wish to continue meeting to study the other guides in this series by Charles
Colson: *Justice* and *Transforming Society.*

Ideas for Group Worship

Sing a hymn like "Where Cross the Crowded Ways of Life,"
"O Zion Haste, Thy Mission High Fulfilling," "Once to
Every Man and Nation," or "Jesus Shall Reign Wher'er the
Sun."

Read Psalm 72 aloud together.

Pray by name for government leaders and for Christians you
know who are involved in the political process. Pray also for the
work of any Christian organizations your group has identified
during your study together.

Reading Resources

Charles Colson, *Kingdoms in Conflict* (New York/Grand Rapids: William Morrow/Zondervan Publishing House, 1987).

Charles Colson, *The Role of The Church in Society* (Wheaton, Ill.: Victor Books, 1986).

Jacques Ellul, *The Political Illusion* (New York: Alfred A. Knopf, 1967).

Paul Marshall, *Thine Is the Kingdom* (Grand Rapids: Eerdmans Publishing Co., 1984).

Richard J. Mouw, *Political Evangelism* (Grand Rapids: Eerdmans Publishing Co., 1973).

Richard John Neuhaus, *The Naked Public Square: Religion and Democracy in America* (Grand Rapids: Eerdmans Publishing Co., 1984).

Arthur Simon, *Christian Faith and Public Policy: No Grounds for Divorce* (Grand Rapids: Eerdmans Publishing Co., 1987).

Notes

SESSION 1: THE COMING OF THE KINGDOM

Charles Colson, *Kingdoms in Conflict* (New York/Grand Rapids: William Morrow/Zondervan Publishing Co., 1987), pages 86-87.

For Further Reflection

John Bright, *The Kingdom of God* (New York and Nashville: Abingdon/Cokesbury, 1953), pages 196-197.

Charles Colson, *Kingdoms in Conflict* (New York/Grand Rapids: William Morrow/Zondervan Publishing Co., 1987), pages 87-88.

Richard J. Mouw, *Political Evangelism* (Grand Rapids: Eerdmans Publishing Co., 1973), page 24.

William Barclay, *The King and His Kingdom* (Philadelphia: Westminster Press, 1968), page 182.

"Charles Colson: Being Christlike in a Worldly Kingdom" in *Charisma and Christian Life,* December 1987, page 30.

SESSION 2: LIVING BETWEEN THE TIMES

Charles Colson, *Kingdoms in Conflict* (New York/Grand Rapids: William Morrow/Zondervan Publishing Co., 1987), pages 83-85.

For Further Reflection

William Barclay, *The King and His Kingdom* (Philadelphia: Westminster Press, 1968), pages 210-211.

Donald Bloesch, *Crumbling Foundations* (Grand Rapids: Zondervan Publishing Co., 1984), page 126.

Richard J. Mouw, *Political Evangelism* (Grand Rapids: Eerdmans Publishing Co., 1973), page 93.

Jacques Ellul, *The Presence of the Kingdom* (New York: Seabury Press, 1948), page 49.

Vernon Grounds, "Bombs or Bibles? Get Ready for Revolution!" in *Christianity Today,* January 15, 1971, page 6.

James W. Skillen, speech entitled "The Bible, Politics and Democracy," Wheaton College, Wheaton, Ill., November 1985.

"Charles Colson: Being Christlike in a Worldly Kingdom" in *Charisma and Christian Life,* December 1987, page 30.

SESSION 3: THE COST OF DISCIPLESHIP

Charles Colson, *Who Speaks for God?* (Westchester, Ill.: Crossway Books, 1985), pages 136-139.

For Further Reflection

Charles Colson, *Loving God* (Grand Rapids: Zondervan Publishing Co., 1983), pages 104-105.

Charles Colson, *Who Speaks for God?* (Westchester, Ill.: Crossway Books, 1985), pages 154-155.

John Stott, *Involvement: Being a Responsible Christian in a Non-Christian Society* (Old Tappan, N.J.: Fleming H. Revell, 1984, 1985), pages 46-47.

Charles Colson, *Who Speaks for God?* (Westchester, Ill.: Crossway Books, 1985), page 145.

SESSION 4: DUAL CITIZENSHIP

Charles Colson, *Kingdoms in Conflict* (New York/Grand Rapids: William Morrow/Zondervan Publishing Co., 1987), pages 89-92.

For Further Reflection

Charles Colson, *Kingdoms in Conflict* (New York/Grand Rapids: William Morrow/Zondervan Publishing Co., 1987), page 94.

Richard J. Neuhaus, speech entitled "The Christian and the Church," Congress on the Bible, Washington, D.C., Fall 1987.

Jacques Ellul, *The Presence of the Kingdom* (New York: Seabury

Press, 1948), page 45.

Donald Bloesch, *Crumbling Foundations* (Grand Rapids: Zondervan Publishing Co., 1984), page 123.

Richard J. Mouw, *Political Evangelism* (Grand Rapids: Eerdmans Publishing Co., 1973), page 55.

SESSION 5: THE CHRISTIAN AND POLITICS

Charles Colson, *Kingdoms in Conflict* (New York/Grand Rapids: William Morrow/Zondervan Publishing Co., 1987), pages 277-279.

For Further Reflection

John Stott, *Involvement: Being a Responsible Christian in a Non-Christian Society* (Old Tappan, N.J.: Fleming H. Revell, 1984, 1985), page 31.

Arthur Simon, *Christian Faith and Public Policy: No Grounds for Divorce* (Grand Rapids: Eerdmans Publishing Co., 1987), page 12.

Charles Colson, *Kingdoms in Conflict* (New York/Grand Rapids: William Morrow/Zondervan Publishing Co., 1987), page 290.

Jacques Ellul, *The Presence of the Kingdom* (New York: Seabury Press, 1948), page 54.

R.C. Sproul, *Life Views: Understanding the Ideas That Shape Society Today* (Old Tappan, N.J.: Fleming H. Revell, 1986), pages 208-209.

Charles Colson, *Kingdoms in Conflict* (New York/Grand Rapids: William Morrow/Zondervan Publishing Co., 1987), pages 289-290.

SESSION 6: THE PARADOX OF POWER

Charles Colson, *Kingdoms in Conflict* (New York/Grand Rapids: William Morrow/Zondervan Publishing Co., 1987), pages 272-274.

For Further Reflection

R.C. Sproul, *Life Views: Understanding the Ideas That Shape Society Today* (Old Tappan, N.J.: Fleming H. Revell, 1986), page 209.

Charles Colson, *The Role of the Church in Society* (Wheaton, Ill.: Scripture Press, 1986), pages 37-38.

Arthur Simon, *Christian Faith and Public Policy: No Grounds for Divorce* (Grand Rapids: Eerdmans Publishing Co., 1987), pages 42-43.

Charles Colson, *Kingdoms in Conflict* (New York/Grand Rapids: William Morrow/Zondervan Publishing Co., 1987), page 88.

Charles Colson, *Kingdoms in Conflict* (New York/Grand Rapids: William Morrow/Zondervan Publishing Co., 1987), pages 303-304.

John Stott, *Involvement: Being a Responsible Christian in a Non-Christian Society* (Old Tappan, N.J.: Fleming H. Revell, 1984, 1985), page 67.

Richard J. Neuhaus, speech entitled "The Christian and the Church," Congress on the Bible, Washington, D.C., Fall 1987.

Peter Berger, "Different Gospels: The Social Sources of Apostasy" in *This World,* Spring 1987, page 15.

Charles Colson, *Kingdoms in Conflict* (New York/Grand Rapids: William Morrow/Zondervan Publishing Co., 1987), page 275.